What Jesus Did

Other titles by Avril Rowlands

All the Tales from the Ark

*The Animals' Caravan: The Journey Begins
**The Animals' Caravan: Stories Jesus Told
***The Animals' Caravan: The Journey Continues
****The Animals' Caravan: Who Jesus Was

Look out for this symbol*. You will find these stories in the earlier books in the series.

The Animals' Caravan

What Jesus Did

Adventures through the Bible
with Caravan Bear and friends

Avril Rowlands
Illustrated by Kay Widdowson

To Nick Wright
With my love and thanks for your friendship and help. A. R.

Text copyright © 2020 Avril Rowlands
Illustrations copyright © 2020 Kay Widdowson
This edition copyright © 2020 Lion Hudson IP Limited

The right of Avril Rowlands to be identified as the author and of Kay Widdowson to be identified as the illustrator of this work has been asserted by them in accordance with the Copyright, Designs and Patents Act 1988.

All rights reserved. No part of this publication may be reproduced or transmitted in any form or by any means, electronic or mechanical, including photocopy, recording, or any information storage and retrieval system, without permission in writing from the publisher.

Published by
Lion Hudson Limited
Wilkinson House, Jordan Hill Business Park,
Banbury Road, Oxford OX2 8DR, England
www.lionhudson.com

ISBN 978 0 7459 7815 4
eISBN 978 0 7459 7816 1

First edition 2020

A catalogue record for this book is available from the British Library

Printed and bound in the UK, April 2020, LH26

Contents

1	Jesus Finds Friends *Luke 5*	7
2	The Wedding at Cana *John 2*	26
3	Teaching the People *Matthew 5–7*	39
4	Feeding Five Thousand *Matthew 14; Mark 6; Luke 9; John 6*	55
5	Walking on Water *Matthew 14*	71
6	Healing the Sick *Mark 7, 8; John 5*	86
7	Raising the Dead *John 11*	104
8	A Meal with Friends *John 21*	120

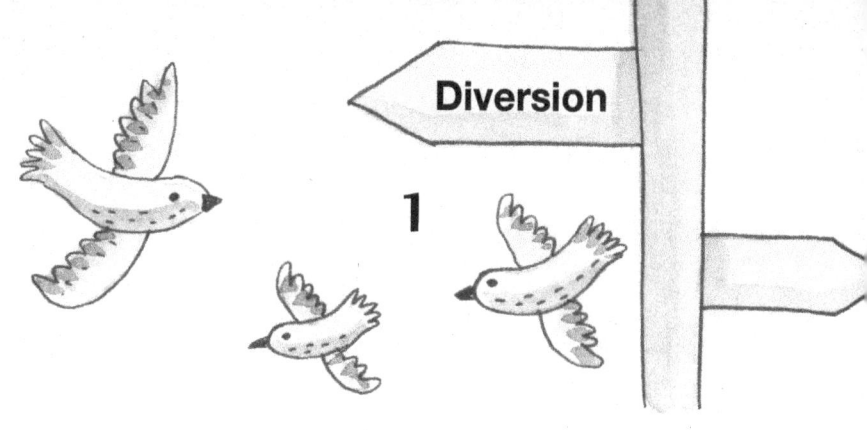

Jesus Finds Friends

Hector the horse stopped abruptly.

"What's the matter, Hector?" asked Caravan Bear, who was sitting on the front step of the caravan.

"Look," said Hector, nodding toward the large red notice with white lettering right in front of him.

The notice read, "ROAD AHEAD CLOSED".

Whitby the dog bounded down. "There's another notice, Hector – down that side road!"

This notice was yellow with black lettering and read "DIVERSION". An arrow pointed the way.

"I hope it doesn't take us a long way around. I'd hate to be late for Christopher Rabbit's birthday," muttered Caravan Bear.

Hector pulled the caravan onto the side road and set off at a trot.

A short while later, he stopped again at another Road Closed notice.

"Where do I go now?" he asked.

"There's an arrow pointing down that lane," Whitby told him.

Hector looked. It was a narrow lane with steep banks and overhanging trees. It had rained recently and the road was wet and slippery. Hector turned into it with a sigh.

He and the caravan were soon spattered with mud.

"And I only washed and polished it this morning," Caravan Bear moaned.

"Me or the caravan?" Hector asked grimly.

"Both," Caravan Bear replied.

Turnings off the lane were blocked by barriers and more Road Closed notices. Other turnings had diversion arrows and Hector grew quite dizzy as he followed these arrows, twisting and turning as he pulled the caravan down one lane after another.

They reached a crossroads and Hector stopped. The three possible roads all had barriers across them and Road Closed signs.

Caravan Bear climbed down and sighed. "I think we've got to turn around," he said. "I'll open that gate over there, and you pull the caravan into the field. You'll be able to turn there."

He swung open the gate and Hector pulled the caravan through... and his hooves sank into a mass of thick, squelchy mud. The caravan shuddered to a halt.

They were well and truly stuck!

* * * * *

Christopher Rabbit looked around his living room with satisfaction. On the mantelpiece were rows of birthday cards, and the table was groaning under the weight of the food he had made for the party. His small bag was packed, ready to leave for another summer of adventure with Caravan Bear, Hector, and Whitby. Most importantly, his Bible was sitting on the hall table.

His Bible. Every time he looked at it, he thought back to the day his life had changed: the day when he had walked out of his burrow in despair because no one had come to his birthday party and he thought he had no friends.

What Jesus Did

He had found the parcel, wrapped in shiny golden paper, lying in the middle of the road. The label on it was addressed to him. He had sat down in the road – which was not a good place to choose to sit – and torn off the wrapping. Inside was a Bible and on the first page was written "Read Me".

He had been sitting staring at it when Hector, towing the caravan, had narrowly missed running him over. Caravan Bear, Whitby, and Hector had invited him to travel with them and their friendship had begun.

Suddenly the doorbell rang. Christopher Rabbit's friends had begun to arrive. Min the cat came first, armed with her knitting. Min knitted scarves, jackets, and both paw and tail warmers for her large family. When they came to visit they always wore her latest present, for they were very fond of Min and didn't like to tell her that they had more than enough knitted clothes.

Susie the squirrel arrived next, then Frank the mole, Lantwit the owl, and many more. Soon Christopher

Rabbit's small room was filled with animals and birds, all eating, talking, and enjoying themselves.

But where were Caravan Bear, Hector, and Whitby? Christopher Rabbit went outside and looked up the road. It was beginning to grow dark. He felt a sinking in his stomach. Perhaps one or other of them was ill? Perhaps they had decided not to come? Perhaps they didn't want to see him?

Christopher Rabbit often found it hard to believe he had such good friends. He was quite a timid rabbit and sometimes wondered whether they would prefer to go away without him but didn't like to tell him. After all, Caravan Bear, Whitby, and Hector had been friends for a long, long time. True, he told them stories from the Bible that they all seemed to enjoy, but still…

Just then Henry the beaver arrived with his family.

"Sorry we're late, Christopher Rabbit. A very happy birthday to you."

"You haven't seen my caravan friends, have you?" Christopher Rabbit asked anxiously. "They should have been here hours ago."

"Hmm," snorted Henry. "I expect they got lost. That's why we're late. Road Closed and Diversion signs all around the village. Wouldn't bother us normally – we'd just squeeze under the signs – but there were so many, we got confused and took the wrong turning."

"*You* got confused, dad," said Tom, one of Henry's sons.

"I blame the weasels, myself," said Maisie, Henry's wife.

"Why?" asked Christopher Rabbit.

"Oh, they probably did it for a joke. They're like that."

"I'll joke *them*," said Henry angrily. "Just wait until I get my paws on them!"

"They might have done it to get their own back when they got tangled up in Min's knitting wool and they ended up in the duck pond," said Jack, the eldest of the beavers' sons. *** "We did laugh, didn't we, lads?"

The beavers' other sons nodded in agreement.

"What can we do?" Christopher Rabbit asked.

"Do? We can't do anything to those weasels until it's daylight," Henry said. "Mind you, I expect they'll have gone to ground by then and we'll have a job finding them."

"I mean *do* about my friends, Caravan Bear, Whitby, and Hector," Christopher Rabbit explained. "We can't just leave them stranded somewhere."

"I'll fly over the village and see if I can spot them," Lantwit offered, and flew off.

When he returned, he was shaking his head. "They're not far away, but the caravan is stuck in a very muddy field."

"Mud?" said Henry. "Mud's no problem for us beavers. Just you leave it to us."

"I'll come with you," said Christopher Rabbit. "After all, they're my friends."

"I'll come too," said Min.

"So will I," said Susie, and in the end everyone at the party set off, armed with torches, spades, ropes, and anything else that might come in useful. Min hastily put a few cakes into a basket in case anyone was hungry.

It took a long time before the caravan was freed, and it was a very tired, very dirty, and very hungry – for the cakes had long since been eaten – group that finally made their way back to Christopher Rabbit's burrow.

Caravan Bear parked the caravan in the garden.

"I'll clean it tomorrow," he promised before following the rest of the animals inside to enjoy hot water, towels, and a lot more food and drink.

"Thank you all for rescuing us," said Caravan Bear gratefully.

"It was a pleasure," smiled Henry. "That's what friends are for."

Everyone nodded agreement.

It was now very late but no one wanted the party to end.

"Would you like me to read you a story from the Bible?" Christopher Rabbit asked shyly.

"An excellent way to finish the evening," said Min briskly, getting out her knitting needles. "Knit one, purl one, knit one…" She was soon engrossed in the complicated knitting pattern. "I *am* listening," she said.

Christopher Rabbit opened the Bible.

"This story is about friends."

He looked around the warm and cosy room. He had made a fire, not because it was cold but because it looked more cheerful. The faces of his friends and neighbours were lit up in its bright blaze.

"I am a lucky rabbit," he thought to himself before starting to read.

"Jesus had a message from God that he knew he had to share. The message, the good news, was something completely new and different from anything anyone had heard before. It was that God loves and cares for each one of us. He started telling people this good news and he began healing sick people. He went to his home in Nazareth, but when he gave them the news, they didn't want to listen and threw him out of the synagogue."

"What's a synagogue?" asked Lantwit.

"It's a place where Jews go to pray to God."

"Why did they throw him out?" Hector asked. He was outside in the garden, his head poking in through the window.

Christopher Rabbit looked at his Bible. "Jesus said that a prophet is never welcomed in his home town."

"I wonder why that is?" Min murmured, turning a corner in the paw warmer she was knitting.

"Do you think it might be because everyone in his village had seen Jesus grow up?" Caravan Bear wondered.

"Dad doesn't think we've grown up," said Jack. He was a large beaver, who towered over his father. "I think he and Mother still think of us as kits."

"What's a 'kit'?" asked Min. "Is it like a kitten?"

"It's a baby beaver," Jack replied.

Everyone was silent for a moment, trying to imagine Jack and his equally big brothers as baby beavers. It wasn't easy.

Christopher Rabbit went on. "Jesus went off to nearby villages, and everyone who heard him was amazed at his teaching and how he was able to heal sick people."

"Does he heal sick animals as well?" Albert, the old, grey badger who lived deep in the forest, stood on the doorstep.

"Come in!" Christopher Rabbit said, getting up and bringing the badger to a place by the fire. "Would you like something to eat?"

"No, thank you," said Albert. "Does this Jesus heal

sick animals as well? Because my arthritis has been something shocking…"

"Jesus lived thousands of years ago," said Whitby scornfully. "And he didn't live anywhere near here…"

Christopher Rabbit interrupted. "Jesus lived *on earth* thousands of years ago, but although we can't see him, he's still here with us."

"Where?" Albert asked, looking around. "My eyesight isn't too good," he explained. "Neither's my hearing, after those people came with loud tractors and chainsaws to cut down the trees. They made a terrible noise – and the mess they left behind…"

"Oh, go on with the story, Christopher Rabbit," said Min impatiently.

"This story is about Jesus finding friends to share his work," Christopher Rabbit explained to Albert. He read on. "One day Jesus was teaching beside a lake. A huge crowd had gathered and he realized that those at the back wouldn't be able to see or hear him.

"He saw two boats moored at the water's edge, which belonged to some fishermen who were washing their nets nearby. Jesus climbed into one of the boats and asked one of the fishermen to push him off from the shore. He wanted to go a little way into the lake so that everyone could see him. Simon, who Jesus called Peter, pushed the boat out, and Jesus sat in it and told the good news to the crowd."

"Did he heal people who were sick from the boat?" asked Albert. "It wouldn't have been easy for sick people to wade through the water to get to him, would it? Especially if they had problems walking. Perhaps they couldn't swim. What about that, eh? They might have drowned or caught a chill.

I remember my old Auntie Gladys – now she was a good age when she died. Well, she fell into a pond, just a little one…"

Susie flicked her tail impatiently.

"I don't know if Jesus healed people from the boat," Christopher Rabbit said hurriedly. "But I'm sure that if he did, the sick people would have been able to get to him. When he'd finished speaking, he told Peter to push the boat further out into deep water so that he and his brother Andrew could let their fishing nets down to catch some fish."

"He probably thought he'd stopped their fishing by taking over the boat," remarked Caravan Bear.

"They might not have had enough fish for supper," said Whitby, who, despite having eaten a lot, was still hungry.

"Fancy eating fish!" said Hector scornfully. "Give me oats and hay, and a nice carrot or apple for dessert, any day," he finished wistfully.

Caravan Bear got up and gave Hector an apple. Hector beamed.

"Have you got any of your elderflower wine?" asked Albert. "I don't know why, but I've got a terrible thirst. Perhaps I've got that nasty thing that killed poor Uncle Joseph. He got this terrible thirst and drank and drank until one day…" He stopped.

"Well?" asked Hector, munching his apple. "What happened?"

"He swelled and he swelled… and then he exploded," said Albert solemnly. He turned to Christopher Rabbit. "Your elderflower wine would go down a treat," he said wistfully, licking his lips.

"I'm really sorry, I don't have any left," Christopher Rabbit apologized. "We drank it all before you came. I've got water…"

"Water!" said Albert dismissively. "Who wants water when they can have elderflower wine!" He blinked a couple of times and stared at Christopher Rabbit as if he suspected him of hiding bottles, then sighed and made for the door.

"Thank you for your hospitality," he said. "But I must be on my way. I can't move like I used to so it'll take me a long time to get home."

With that, he went out the door.

"Oh dear," sighed Christopher Rabbit.

"He's a really miserable animal," said Susie.

"Well, he's old and doesn't have any friends…" Christopher Rabbit began.

"And why's that?" asked Susie. "It's because he's always talking about himself."

"Go on with the story," urged Whitby.

"All right," said Christopher Rabbit, "although I wish I had some elderflower wine. Albert is difficult, but I do feel sorry for him."

"I can't remember where you got up to," Maisie said.

Christopher Rabbit looked down at his Bible. "Jesus had just told Peter and Andrew to row further out and let down their nets. Peter shook his head. 'We've been out all night long and caught nothing. But we'll have another go if you want.'

"So they rowed further out and let down the nets and, to their amazement, they caught so many fish that their nets were about to break into holes under the weight. Two other brothers, James and John, hurriedly climbed into their boat and rowed out to help, and they all caught so many fish that the boats seemed likely to sink."

"Could they swim?" asked Hector.

"Who? The fish?" Whitby asked innocently. Hector shook his head at her.

"The fishermen didn't need to," Christopher Rabbit replied. "When they'd rowed back to shore, Jesus said to them, 'From now on, I'll teach you how to fish for people – to teach them about God. Follow me!' The fishermen pulled their boats high up onto the beach, left them there, and followed Jesus."

"What, they left all that catch of fish behind?" asked Maisie, slightly shocked.

"I don't know," Christopher Rabbit replied. "It doesn't say. Perhaps they sold the fish or gave them away before following Jesus."

"If they just left the fish behind, I call it wasteful," Maisie retorted, shaking her head.

"Doesn't the story mean that they thought what Jesus was saying and doing was more important than just being fishermen?" asked Caravan Bear.

"I think so," Christopher Rabbit agreed. "Jesus chose twelve people altogether to be his special friends – his disciples. They were quite a mixed bunch – some were rich, some were poor, but they all followed Jesus and began to learn the good news about the kingdom of God."

He closed the Bible and looked around at his friends. Min had stopped knitting and her eyes were half closed. Henry's eyes were fully closed and he was beginning to snore. It was as if they had all suddenly realized how very tired they were. No one made a move to go.

"You're all welcome to stay," Christopher Rabbit said. No one answered. He went into his bedroom and climbed into bed.

"Thank you, God, for my friends," he said quietly. "Thank you for their help in finding the caravan. We all need friends. I'm sorry Albert doesn't have any. Perhaps you can help him find some."

And he closed his eyes and was soon fast asleep.

The Wedding at Cana

The day after Christopher Rabbit's birthday was a busy one.

He spent the morning clearing up after saying goodbye to the friends who had spent the night sleeping on the floor of his burrow.

Caravan Bear spent the morning washing and grooming Hector before cleaning the mud off the outside of the caravan and polishing its wheels.

Hector – after being washed and groomed – spent the morning relaxing in Christopher Rabbit's garden, quietly munching the grass.

Whitby spent the morning running around. Her offer to help Christopher Rabbit was politely turned down after she had accidentally broken a glass, and her offer to help Caravan Bear was also turned down after she had knocked a bucket of water over Hector.

"When are we going off on our adventures?" she asked Caravan Bear.

"Soon," Caravan Bear replied.

"You said that an hour ago," Whitby retorted.

Hector raised his head. "We're already having adventures," he said. "Yesterday was one. Not that it was a nice adventure, but it was an adventure all the same."

"But I want to go away!" cried Whitby.

"We *are* away," Caravan Bear said. "We're not at home, we're at Christopher Rabbit's, and as soon as the caravan is clean, Hector is rested, and Christopher Rabbit has cleared up, we'll be off."

"Here, there, wherever the fancy takes us!" Whitby shouted, waving her tail.

"Exactly."

"But when?"

Caravan Bear was saved from answering by the arrival of Henry, Maisie, and their sons. Henry was smiling and rubbing his paws together.

"That's properly sorted those weasels," he grinned.

"What do you mean?" asked Caravan Bear.

"Caught in the act, you might say. We spotted them moving those road signs around."

"What did you do?" Whitby asked eagerly. "Did you lock them up?"

Henry the beaver was a very important animal in the village, who had been put in charge of locking up bad animals.

"No need," he replied. "I just gave them a piece of my mind, then Maisie here gave them a piece of *her* mind, then some of the motorists who'd got lost gave them a piece of *their* minds. Then we made them remove all the signs. Then we took them home, where their mothers gave them such a telling off – it was good to see."

"Did they say they were sorry?" asked Christopher Rabbit, coming out of his burrow with a duster in his paw.

"No, but I don't think you'll have any more trouble from them," Henry said with confidence.

"I wouldn't be so sure," Maisie sniffed. "Trouble with you, Henry, is that you're too trusting."

"Well, I like to see the good in animals," Henry replied tolerantly. "There's good in most of them somewhere."

"Somewhere so deep down that it can be hard to find," said Maisie. "Well, they're only young weasels and I hope they've learned their lesson. Anyway, we've brought a hamper of food, Christopher Rabbit, seeing as we ate everything in your larder. Or rather, my greedy sons did."

As it was a fine day, they had a picnic lunch on the lawn. After eating everything that Maisie had brought, no one felt like doing any more work that day.

"Would you tell us about some of the things Jesus did?" Caravan Bear asked Christopher Rabbit. "You said that he taught people about God and healed the sick."

"He also performed miracles," Christopher Rabbit replied.

"What's a miracle?" asked Maisie.

"I think it's something that happens that's out of the ordinary and can only be done by God."

"Tell us about one," said Whitby, running to fetch Christopher Rabbit's Bible.

Christopher Rabbit opened the book.

"This is the first miracle that Jesus performed. It happened in a town called Cana. Jesus' mother was there…"

"That was Mary, wasn't it?" asked Whitby.

"That's right. It was a wedding, and Jesus and some of his friends had been invited."

"Whose wedding was it?" asked Maisie.

"I don't know," Christopher Rabbit replied. "It might have been the wedding of a relative or family friend, because Mary seems to have been involved in organizing it."

"These things take a lot of organizing," said Whitby, nodding her head wisely.

"How would you know?" asked Hector. "I bet you've never organized a wedding – or a party, come to that."

"Your birthday party must have taken a lot of organizing," Caravan Bear said to Christopher Rabbit. "I'm sorry we missed it."

The Wedding at Cana

"You didn't miss it," replied Christopher Rabbit earnestly. "It was a bit like having two parties. The first one was before we all went to find you, and the second was after we found you." He thought for a moment. "It was a very special party and I'll never forget it."

"If only because we ate all your food and drank all your drink," remarked Henry.

Christopher Rabbit looked down at his Bible. "That's also what happened at the wedding at Cana. They ran out of wine."

"Poor old Alfred," said Maisie. "You know he only came because of your elderflower wine, Christopher Rabbit? You hadn't sent him an invitation, had you?"

Christopher Rabbit shook his head.

"Who wants *him* at a party?" said Tom, dismissively. "Miserable old badger!"

"Go on with the story," Whitby demanded.

"I should have sent him an invitation, though," Christopher Rabbit said thoughtfully. "He's old and probably lonely."

"I want to hear about the miracle," Whitby insisted.

Christopher Rabbit started to read. "When they

ran out of wine, Jesus' mother caught hold of her son. 'There isn't any left,' she told him."

"What did she expect Jesus to do about it?" asked Hector. "Go to the nearest supermarket and buy some?"

"Why not?" said Maisie. "You said Cana was a town, didn't you? Well, towns have supermarkets and shops, don't they?"

"They might have been closed," Caravan Bear said. "And anyway, I don't think they had shops like we do. It was a long time ago."

"I don't think Mary meant going off to the shops," Christopher Rabbit said, wrinkling up his nose. "I think she knew that Jesus could do something extraordinary."

"Did she know that he was God's Son?" Caravan Bear asked.

Christopher Rabbit thought for a moment.

"Yes," he said at last. "Because, if you remember, an angel had visited her and told her that God had chosen her to be the mother of his Son." **

"So what did Jesus say?" asked Caravan Bear.

"He told his mother that his time hadn't come yet," Christopher Rabbit went on.

"What did that mean?" Henry asked.

"I don't really know," Christopher Rabbit replied. "Perhaps he was waiting for a sign from God."

"But he'd had a sign from God already, hadn't he?" Caravan Bear said. "Don't you remember, when he was baptized, a dove flew down and rested on him. And God said that Jesus was his Son, whom he loved." ****

Hector nodded his head. "I'd have said that was a pretty definite sign from God."

"Well, perhaps he thought that now he had to take his orders straight from God and not from his mother," Henry wondered.

"Maybe. But his mother obviously thought differently, because she turned to the servants and told them to do whatever Jesus wanted," Christopher Rabbit replied.

"You just listen to that, boys," Maisie told her sons. "Mother knows best."

"Jesus told them to fill six large stone jars with water. The jars were used for washing the feet of the guests. The servants filled them to the brim. Then Jesus told one of them to draw some of the water from one of the jars and give it to the chief steward. The servant did that. And as he began to pour the water into a cup, he realized that it had been changed into a rich wine."

"Not elderflower wine," said Whitby mischievously.

Christopher Rabbit blushed. "It doesn't say what sort of wine it was in the Bible," he said.

"We could have done with a miracle like that yesterday," Hector remarked. "Then Alfred wouldn't have had anything to complain about."

Christopher Rabbit continued. "The chief steward didn't know where the wine had come from. He went to the bridegroom and said, 'Everyone else serves the best wine first, then when the guests have had plenty to drink, the ordinary, cheaper wine is served. But you've kept the best wine until last!'"

He closed the Bible and everyone was silent for a moment, thinking about the story.

"So that was the first miracle?" asked Whitby. She sounded disappointed.

Christopher Rabbit nodded.

"It was a very small miracle though, wasn't it?" Whitby said. "As it was the first one, I thought Jesus would have done something really big – some sort of huge, exciting miracle."

"That's what you'd have done, is it?" asked Hector, amused.

"Well, yes," said Whitby. "I think Jesus should have performed a miracle to make everyone sit up and think, 'Wow, this really is God's Son.'"

"Oh, I don't know," said Caravan Bear. "Doesn't it show that God looks after small things as well as big ones?"

"But all it did was save the bride's family from being upset and embarrassed," said Whitby firmly.

"And what's wrong with that?" asked Caravan Bear.

"I don't think Jesus went in for doing big, showy things," said Christopher Rabbit slowly.

Maisie turned to her four sons. "I hope you've been listening to that story, boys. There's a good lesson there, and that's to trust your mother and always do what she says," she stated firmly.

"All right, Mother," said Tom. "You've made your point."

"I think that story also tells us to trust God, who wants the best for us in small things as well as in big things," Christopher Rabbit said.

Henry cleared his throat. "Time we were off," he said. "Farmer Jones has asked us to tidy up a stream

The Wedding at Cana

that's been flooding his field."

The beavers said goodbye and left.

"And it's time we were off, isn't it?" Whitby asked anxiously.

"We'll go first thing in the morning," Caravan Bear said firmly. "Christopher Rabbit must be worn out from cleaning and then reading us a story. And I wouldn't mind having a rest."

"Me too," Hector agreed.

Whitby looked disappointed.

"Let's think of this as the first real night of our holiday," Caravan Bear said, looking at Whitby's disappointed face. "I'll get my guitar and we'll sing."

He looked at Christopher Rabbit. "You'll spend the night with us in the caravan, won't you?"

"Once I've made sure everything's tidied away," Christopher Rabbit replied.

Caravan Bear fetched his guitar, sat on the top step of the caravan, and began to play while Christopher Rabbit went back to his burrow. When he was satisfied that his home was clean and tidy, he picked up his small bag and turned to go.

"Thank you, God, for the miracle Jesus performed at the wedding, and for the loving way he helped that family," he said out loud.

Then he stepped outside, closed the door, and went to join his friends.

Teaching the People

"There are eyes in those bushes," Whitby whispered. "I'm scared."

"Of course there aren't," Caravan Bear said briskly. "You're imagining things."

Christopher Rabbit, sitting on the step with Caravan Bear and Whitby, had also seen the eyes. He was scared too but didn't want to admit it.

They had been travelling all day, and the sun was now beginning to set as Hector towed the caravan along a road through a thick forest. Caravan Bear had hoped to be clear of the woods before stopping for the night, but Hector refused to tow the caravan in the dark, so they would soon have to find somewhere to park.

Caravan Bear liked forests but even he had to admit that this one was – well, a bit frightening. The trees were so very old and had been planted so very close together that it seemed darker than it really was.

Christopher Rabbit nudged him. "Just look at that grass."

Caravan Bear looked. The grass verges on either side of the road had been ripped up and there were deep holes in the turf. Many of the trees had long raking scratches up their sides. He shivered.

This forest was an altogether strange and unfriendly place. There was no bird song, no squeakings, rustlings, or murmurs of woodland creatures going about their business. Apart from the sound of Hector's clop-clopping hooves, it was silent.

Seeing a small patch of open ground surrounded by thick gorse bushes, Hector pulled onto it with a sigh.

"That's it," he said. "I'm tired and it's nearly dark and I'm stopping here for the night."

"Can't we ride on a bit, just until we get out of this wood?" asked Whitby. "I don't like it."

"No, we can't," Hector replied stubbornly.

Teaching the People

"A wood is a wood. Nothing to be afraid of."

He dropped his head and began to graze.

Caravan Bear and Christopher Rabbit jumped down from the caravan steps and started to set up.

They were stopped by the sound of snuffling and grunting. The gorse bushes shook and two very large pig-like creatures with rough brown hair, thick, razor-sharp tusks, and small eyes came out into the open. They were wild pigs, called boars.

"Hello," Christopher Rabbit said nervously.

The boars stared at the caravan for a long moment without speaking.

"These are *our* woods," one of them said at last.

"Didn't you see our marks?" the other boar asked.

"What marks?" asked Caravan Bear.

"The scratches on the trees," Bruce, the first boar, replied.

"The turf ploughed up and ripped to shreds," Boris, the second boar, grinned, showing his sharp teeth.

"That's what we do to animals who come into *our* woods without permission," said Bruce, pushing his snout close to Caravan Bear's face. "This is the Wild Wood and you've pitched your caravan right in the middle of it."

"I see," said Caravan Bear, moving back a step or two. "How do we get permission?"

The boars looked at one another.

"You ask for it," said Bruce. "But that doesn't mean you get it," he added with a snuffling laugh.

"We don't take kindly to strangers." Boris sniggered. "Made mincemeat of the last lot."

"Yes, I mean, no. I do understand," said Caravan Bear, trying not to show how scared he was.

The boars walked slowly round and round the caravan without speaking. Caravan Bear, Christopher Rabbit, and Hector watched them fearfully, while Whitby crept underneath.

"If," Bruce said at last, "and it's a big if, we allow you to stay for the night…"

"…without ripping you and your caravan to shreds…" Boris added.

"…you'll have to entertain us," finished Bruce.

Caravan Bear frowned. "Entertain you? How?"

"The last visitors sang and danced, but we didn't like it…" Bruce said.

"So we…" Boris grinned evilly.

"What can you do?" interrupted Bruce.

"Well… I play the guitar…" Caravan Bear began.

"And Christopher Rabbit tells stories." Whitby added, coming out from his hiding place.

The boars looked at Christopher Rabbit.

"Stories? What sort of stories?" Bruce demanded.

"F-from the Bible," Christopher Rabbit stammered.

What Jesus Did

The boars looked at one another and nodded.

"All right," said Bruce. "You tell us a story and if we like it, you can stay for the night. If we don't…"

They grinned and began to move away.

"We'll be back," Boris said, and they disappeared into the wood.

"Can't we get away?" asked Whitby urgently.

A gorse bush quivered and Bruce came out.

"Don't even think about it," he said. "You're surrounded." He retreated through the bushes.

The friends ate a hurried meal while Christopher Rabbit looked through the stories in the Bible and tried to decide which one would entertain the boars. He shuddered at the thought of those dangerous tusks.

"Please, God, help me," he muttered. "What shall I read?"

He still hadn't decided by the time the gorse bushes quivered and the boars returned. They were followed by others, including one very large, old one.

"My mother," Boris said. "Her name's Bertha. She's very hard to please."

Bertha nodded.

"Right, rabbit," she said in a gravelly voice. "You can begin."

Christopher Rabbit took a deep breath and opened the Bible on a random page. He looked down and gulped. Perhaps this wouldn't be the best story to read to a group of dangerous boars. He cleared his throat.

"This is about what Jesus taught to his friends and to the crowds who came to listen to him," he began.

"Who's Jesus?" interrupted Boris.

"He's God's Son," Caravan Bear replied.

The boars looked at one another.

"Do you know who God is?" Christopher Rabbit asked nervously.

"You think we're stupid or something?" Bertha asked. "Of course we know who God is!"

WHAT JESUS DID

"We're among the cleverest animals on earth," boasted Boris.

"And the most dangerous," Bruce added.

"Oh. Right." Christopher Rabbit gulped and read on. "Well, when Jesus saw the crowds, he went up a hill and sat down. His disciples joined him and he began to teach them about God and what God wants us to be like."

"Was that a bit like Moses, and the ten

commandments he brought down the mountain from God?" Hector asked. ***

Hector didn't seem troubled by the boars. Whitby wondered if it was because he could run faster than them.

Christopher Rabbit thought for a moment. "Perhaps. Although the ten commandments was more of a list of things people should or shouldn't do. I think Jesus' teaching was about blessings – being in a loving relationship with God and with everyone else."

"You mean, being friends with God?" asked Bruce.

"Well, yes."

"Boars don't make friends," Bruce said firmly. "Not with God, not with anyone."

"Jesus explained that God was good and loving and wants us, his creatures, to be good and loving to each other," Christopher Rabbit went on.

"Was he serious?" asked Boris, disbelievingly.

Christopher Rabbit continued nervously. "He told them that we should be satisfied with what we have and share what we have with others."

Bertha stirred. "If we did that, we wouldn't have enough for ourselves," she said. "It stands to reason."

"Jesus said that we shouldn't worry about the clothes we wear or the food we eat as God will provide everything we need."

"Huh! If we didn't worry about food, we'd starve," said Bertha sourly. "I don't think much of this story."

The boars muttered, and the friends looked at each other and wondered when the boars would start attacking them.

"Go on," said Bertha, waving her great tusks in the air. "What else did Jesus say?"

Christopher Rabbit took a deep breath. "He said blessed are the meek, for they will inherit the earth."

Bertha laughed. "You can't be meek to survive in the Wild Wood. You have to be tough. This is our land and only we boars will have it. My sons fight first and asks questions afterward." She thought for a moment. "That's if there's anyone left to answer them."

Christopher Rabbit swallowed. "Jesus said that if we don't judge others, then God won't judge us. He said we should forgive others and we'll be forgiven,"

"He said that?" asked Boris.

"If we did that, we'd all be dead," Bertha grunted.

The other boars murmured agreement, their wicked-looking tusks glinting in the moonlight.

"I think Jesus was saying that we should treat others as we'd like them to treat us," Christopher Rabbit went on hurriedly.

Bruce trundled up to Christopher Rabbit and stood over him menacingly.

"Don't you know, little rabbit, that the law of the jungle is to eat or be eaten?"

"But we're not in the jungle," Hector murmured quietly. "Or maybe we are," he added. Fortunately, the boars didn't hear him.

Christopher Rabbit shrank back but said determinedly, "Jesus told us that there is another way, a better way."

The boars were silent for a moment.

"God looks deep into our hearts and knows what we're thinking," Christopher Rabbit went on. "He doesn't just want us to be right on the outside, he wants us to be right inside as well. He said that the really happy creatures are the ones who love God and love their neighbour."

"Who cares about being happy?" asked Bruce. "Being top hog is the most important thing in life."

"That sounds like Runt," Whitby muttered. Bruce turned to her.

"He's a pig we've met," Whitby explained nervously. "He's runs the pig farm for the farmer."

"Pigs!" said Bruce dismissively. "Pathetic creatures! All they're good for is as food for humans. We boars are different."

The other boars nodded and grunted agreement.

"Jesus said that the ones who try to make peace and not fight are the happy ones," Christopher Rabbit pressed on.

"So how does this Jesus know what God wants?" asked Bertha.

"He knows because he's God's Son," Caravan Bear repeated patiently.

"It's the same as if God were saying those things," Hector added.

The boars looked at each other.

"And Jesus said that we should be willing to stand up for God's laws, even if it gets you into trouble or others don't like it…" Christopher Rabbit looked up, which wasn't a good idea, for the circle of boars all staring at him looked very menacing. He stopped speaking.

"Well, I'll say this for you, rabbit," Bertha said after a long silence. "You're pretty brave to tell us all this."

"I'm not at all brave," Christopher Rabbit explained. "I'm actually very timid. If I seem at all brave, it's because I asked God for help." He took a deep breath, knowing that what he said next might make the boars very angry indeed but feeling that he had to say it.

"When we came into this forest, it was very dark and very quiet. There aren't any birds singing or sounds of other animals. Is that because you scare them away?" he asked.

Bertha laughed. "Too right," she agreed.

"Perhaps," Christopher Rabbit went on recklessly, "perhaps if you didn't frighten them but welcomed them into your wood and and tried to make friends with them, you might find you get on…" His voice trailed away.

There was a moment of horrible silence. The boars looked at one another.

"I don't think we can go as far as that," Bertha said at last. She nodded to Christopher Rabbit. "But it was a good try."

She turned to look at Caravan Bear, Hector, and Whitby. "You can all stay in our wood tonight."

"Thank you," said Caravan Bear, breathing a huge sigh of relief.

"But only for tonight," warned Bertha, leading the boars away.

For a while no one spoke.

"Phew!" said Whitby at last.

"Well, we wanted adventures," Hector said, before moving to a patch of grass that looked tasty and not too churned up. He began to graze.

"I'm not sure I like adventures like that," said Christopher Rabbit, closing the Bible.

"You don't think they'll come back in the night, do you?" Whitby asked anxiously.

"I don't know. I don't think so," Christopher Rabbit said slowly. "All I do know is that I've got God to thank for giving me the strength to tell that story."

He closed his eyes for a moment. He still felt weak and a bit shaky. "Thank you, God, for protecting us. Help us to rely on you always and especially when we're scared." He opened his eyes and looked at the others. "Perhaps some of what Jesus taught will make the boars think."

"And the Wild Wood won't be as wild in future," said Whitby.

"Let's hope so," agreed Christopher Rabbit.

Feeding Five Thousand

Christopher Rabbit looked up when he heard a gate open. He shaded his eyes from the sun and saw Caravan Bear, weighed down by heavy bags of shopping, close the gate and cross the meadow toward him.

"You should have let me come with you," he called, jumping down the caravan steps and running to take one of the bags. "I've just been sitting in the sun, reading the Bible."

"I enjoyed it," Caravan Bear replied. "I've bought lots of food so we shan't go hungry." He looked around. "Where are Whitby and Hector?"

Christopher Rabbit took the shopping from him and carried it into the caravan.

"They've gone fishing," he called through the open door. "At least, Whitby has gone fishing and persuaded Hector to carry the fishing gear."

Caravan Bear frowned. "I hope she hasn't taken my best rod. Anyway, there's no river around here."

"Whitby said there's a pond at the bottom of the meadow," Christopher Rabbit replied. "Shall we go and find them?"

They heard the noise long before they reached the pond.

Caravan Bear sighed. "Now what's happened?"

They hurried forward and arrived in time to see Whitby and a duck tugging hard at something on the ground. The noise came from a crowd of other

ducks on the pond who were clucking and squawking. Hector stood close by, neighing with laughter.

"It's mine!" Whitby growled. "I caught it!"

The duck gave one strong tug and Whitby toppled over backward. The duck flew into the air.

"Give it back!" yelled Whitby.

"Too late!" shouted the duck. "I've swallowed it!"

"Thief!" Whitby called.

"You're the thief," the duck retorted. "It's our duck pond and the fish in it belong to us ducks!"

"Ducks don't eat fish!" Whitby called.

"Yes, we do! We eat little fish. And that was a little fish!"

"It wasn't a little fish! It was a big fish!" Whitby yelled.

"Just a tiddler. A tiny little tiddler!" the duck taunted, flying round and round Whitby's head, while the other ducks cheered and flapped their wings.

"Come on, Whitby," Caravan Bear called. "It's too late to do anything now."

"He ate my fish," Whitby said hotly. "I've never caught a fish before and that greedy duck has eaten it!"

"Well, it is *their* pond," Christopher Rabbit pointed out mildly.

"It's not fair, it's just NOT FAIR!" Whitby retorted, and ran off.

Caravan Bear sighed. "And she took my best rod, too. I hope she hasn't damaged it."

When he, Hector, and Christopher Rabbit returned to the caravan, they found Whitby sulking underneath.

Hector wandered off to the far side of the field while Caravan Bear and Christopher Rabbit prepared a tasty meal.

"Don't want any," Whitby muttered from under the caravan when Caravan Bear tried coaxing her out.

"But it's fish," Caravan Bear tempted. "Your favourite."

Whitby sniffed. "Won't be as nice as the fish I caught."

"Oh, I don't know," Hector replied. He had wandered back to the caravan in the hope that Caravan Bear had bought a few apples for him. "I expect the fish you caught wouldn't have tasted very nice. The pond was muddy and full of nasty-looking green stuff."

"How would you know? You don't eat fish," Whitby retorted.

"And it was only a very *little* fish," Hector said, grinning. "It wouldn't have made a very big meal."

"It made a meal for the duck," Whitby retorted, "And it wasn't a little fish!"

Hector hummed to himself and began grazing on the lush grass.

"Don't tease her," Caravan Bear said. "I remember how proud I was when I caught my first fish."

"Were you?" Whitby asked.

"Oh yes. And if you come and eat your supper, we'll go fishing again soon – and you can catch enough for a meal for all of us."

"Hector doesn't eat fish," Whitby muttered, creeping out from under the caravan. She was beginning to feel very hungry and all the talk of food didn't help.

"Just think what he's missing," Caravan Bear said. Hector smiled.

"I was just reading a story about fish," Christopher Rabbit told Whitby. "You'll like it. I'll read it to you after supper."

So after their meal, Christopher Rabbit brought out his Bible. As it was a fine, warm evening, he, Caravan Bear, Whitby, and Hector settled down outside.

"Everywhere Jesus went, large crowds followed him," Christopher Rabbit began. "There were sick people, wanting Jesus to heal them, and others who wanted him to tell them more about God. Jesus' friends, his disciples, had also been teaching and, when they met up again afterward, Jesus saw that they were tired and hungry."

"I'm sorry I took your best rod, Caravan Bear," Whitby said. She was feeling a bit ashamed of the fuss she had made. "I didn't break it, did I?"

"No," Caravan Bear replied.

"And we can go fishing soon, can't we?"

"Of course."

Whitby was satisfied and settled back to hear the story.

"Jesus and his disciples met by a lake," Christopher Rabbit continued. "They climbed into one of their fishing boats and rowed to a quiet spot on the far shore. But the crowds had hurried around and were waiting for the boat to pull up."

"Jesus must have been like a pop star," Whitby said thoughtfully. "Rather like the story you told us about the crowds who cheered Jesus when he entered Jerusalem."

"On a donkey," added Hector, disapprovingly. ****

Christopher Rabbit nodded. "He felt sorry for the crowds who wanted to see and hear him so much. They were, he thought, like sheep without a shepherd. So he carried on teaching them."

"He must have been tired, too," Whitby added.

Christopher Rabbit nodded. "I expect he was, but I don't think he thought about himself. It was late in the afternoon and Jesus began to worry about all the people. His disciples were worried as well. 'It's very late and this is a lonely spot,' one of them said. 'Send them away so that they can go and buy something to eat.' But Jesus didn't do that. He said, 'You give them something to eat.'"

"How many people were there?" asked Whitby.

Christopher Rabbit looked at the Bible.

"It says that there were five thousand," he replied.

"Five thousand?" squeaked Whitby. "Wow!"

"How did they know it was five thousand?" Hector asked practically. "Did someone count them?"

"Perhaps one of the disciples did," Caravan Bear suggested.

"Well, there were probably a lot more people, as the Bible says that there were five thousand men," Christopher Rabbit explained. "There must have been women and children as well."

"Double wow!" Whitby exclaimed.

"What did the disciples say?" Hector asked.

"They said that feeding that number would take a lot of money," Christopher Rabbit replied. "Jesus told them to find out how many loaves of bread there were. The disciples asked around and came back with just five loaves and two fish."

"Surely the disciples had come with their own food?" Caravan Bear asked.

Christopher Rabbit shook his head. "I don't know."

"If they hadn't, it was a bit silly of them," Caravan Bear said. "You should always be prepared."

"I expect they had more important things to do," Hector interrupted.

Caravan Bear frowned. "Well, I knew we didn't have any food, but as we passed a supermarket on our way, I wasn't worried."

"It's because you plan ahead," said Whitby.

"That's all very well, but some things you can't plan for," Hector argued.

"What sort of things?" Caravan Bear asked.

"If you'd spent the day talking to well over five thousand people, to say nothing of making sick people better, you might have forgotten to go to the supermarket," Hector replied reasonably. "And besides, didn't Christopher Rabbit tell us that God said we weren't to worry about the clothes we wore or the food we ate as God would provide?" Hector continued triumphantly. "That doesn't apply to me, of course, as I don't wear clothes and I can eat anywhere, provided there's grass."

"If I hadn't gone shopping today, none of us, apart from you, would have been able to eat the large meal we've just had," Caravan Bear said stubbornly.

"Pity about Whitby's fish," Hector murmured. "If the duck hadn't nabbed it, you could all have eaten that. It wouldn't have gone very far, though."

Whitby barked at him.

"All I'm trying to say is that God might provide, but surely he expects us to do some work as well," Caravan Bear argued. "It's all right for you, Hector, but the rest of us can't eat grass."

"I'm not sure God was saying that we should sit back and food will drop into our laps, but perhaps that there's plenty of food for everyone if we share it," Christopher Rabbit said thoughtfully.

Caravan Bear frowned. "Perhaps you're right. Now, let me get this straight. There were thousands of people somewhere out in the countryside, miles from anywhere. It was getting late and they were hungry, and all there was to eat were five loaves and two fish?"

Christopher Rabbit nodded. "That's right."

"I wonder if they were big fish or little ones, like Whitby's," Hector teased.

"I think we've heard enough about Whitby's fish," Caravan Bear said firmly.

Hector grinned. "With all those hungry people and pretty much no food, there could have been a riot," he commented.

"Time for a miracle," Whitby said happily.

"That makes Jesus sound like a magician who can wave a wand and make a rabbit come out of a hat," frowned Caravan Bear.

Christopher Rabbit looked confused. "I've never come out of a hat," he said.

"Not you, Christopher Rabbit. It's the sort of thing magicians do," Caravan Bear explained.

"The miracles Jesus did came from God," Christopher Rabbit explained. "They weren't magicians' tricks."

Hector looked up. "But magicians' tricks are all pretend, aren't they?" he asked. "The magician probably swaps hats while no one's looking, an empty one for one with the rabbit inside. Or there's a puff of smoke to hide when the rabbit climbs into the hat. It's not the real thing at all."

"I wouldn't like to be a magician's rabbit," said Christopher Rabbit seriously. "It doesn't sound much fun."

"Not as much fun as having adventures in the caravan with your friends and telling us about God," Caravan Bear said, smiling at him.

Christopher Rabbit felt warm inside.

"So what happened next?" Whitby urged.

"Jesus told the disciples to get the people to sit down in groups on the grass. He took the loaves and the fish and thanked God for the food. He began breaking the bread and dividing the fish, giving it to the disciples to hand around the crowd. And there was plenty for everyone. So much so that there was lots of food left over."

Feeding Five Thousand

"Hold on a minute," Hector said. "Perhaps it wasn't a miracle at all. Might it just have been that people had brought food with them but didn't want to share it until someone offered their five loaves and two fish? Then, feeling a bit ashamed of themselves, they decided to bring out their own food and share it around."

Christopher Rabbit shook his head. "It doesn't say that in the Bible. It says that Jesus took the loaves and

the fish, thanked God for them, then broke them up into bits and gave them to the disciples to hand around. If the people shared their own food with each other it would have been good, but it's not the same as the miracle Jesus performed."

Everyone was silent for a while.

"You know what it reminds me of," Caravan Bear said thoughtfully. "It reminds me of that story you told us about God feeding the Israelites in the desert when Moses had taken them out of slavery in Egypt." ***

"When God gave them a sort of honey cake, and quails?" Whitby asked.

"That's right," Christopher Rabbit agreed. "I think it shows that God cares for people."

"And animals," Whitby said.

"And everything in the world," Caravan Bear added.

"Perhaps, with God's love, we'll always be given enough of what we need," Christopher Rabbit said thoughtfully. He closed the Bible. "Thank you, God, for the miracle of the loaves and fish. Thank you for showing us that food is a gift from you and we should share it with others."

"Even ducks," Hector added.

"All right, Hector. You've made your point," sighed Caravan Bear.

Everyone laughed, even Whitby.

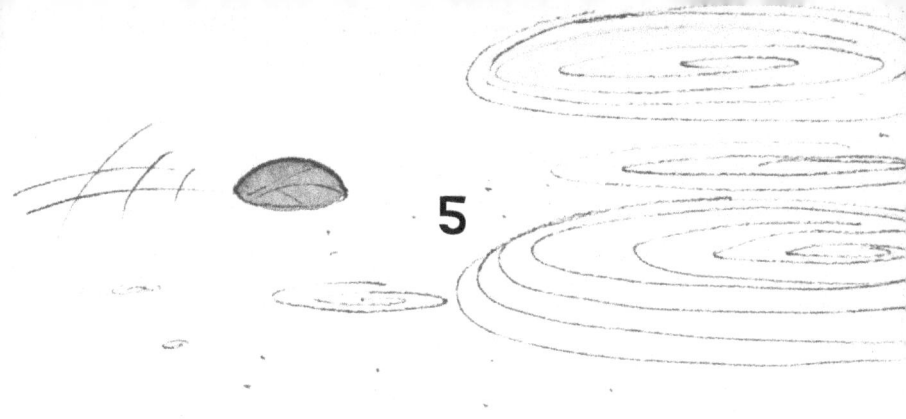

5

Walking on Water

"What a lovely day," Christopher Rabbit said as he looked out over the calm blue sea, which was twinkling and gleaming in the bright sunshine. He picked up a pebble from the small pile beside him and sent it skimming across the water.

He, Caravan Bear, and Whitby were sitting on the edge of a short jetty beside a pebbly beach.

Whitby sent another pebble skimming.

"Mine went furthest!" she shouted.

"This isn't a competition," Caravan Bear commented.

Hector, quietly grazing on the grassy bank beside the beach, smiled to himself.

"Anyway, it's too hot to do anything strenuous," Caravan Bear said. He shaded his eyes and gazed into the distance. "That boat has been there for ages. I don't suppose he'll catch many fish in this heat."

"Why not?" Whitby asked.

"If the fish have any sense, they'll have gone a long way down into the water to keep cool."

They all stared at the tiny boat.

"The sea's so calm you feel you could almost walk across to the boat, just like Jesus did," Christopher Rabbit remarked.

"Did he?" Caravan Bear asked.

Before Christopher Rabbit could reply, they heard a loud honking of a horn followed by a screech of tyres.

"Found you at last!" came a cheerful voice.

Whitby looked around.

"Runt!" she said angrily. "Just when we were enjoying ourselves!"

Caravan Bear laughed. "Oh, Runt's all right," he said tolerantly. He stood up and turned around.

A large pig, looking very hot in an old leather jacket, crash helmet, and goggles, climbed stiffly off an ancient motorbike.

"Hello, Runt. Have you been looking for us?"

"Thought you might like to see my latest bike," Runt said, taking off his goggles and helmet.

"*Your* latest bike?" Hector queried.

"Well, not mine exactly. Mr Doggins bought it."

"I thought the farmer wasn't going to get another one after you had a crash with the first," Whitby said. ****

"Well no, he wasn't, but Mrs Doggins persuaded him," Runt replied. "She told him he needed a bike. She said walking wasn't good for him on account of his bad back. He said all right, but it would have to be an old one. Very mean with his money is Mr Doggins."

"And did he say you could ride it?" asked Hector gently.

"Not in so many words, but Mrs Doggins said it would be all right." He beamed around at them. "She likes me," he added simply. "Told me I'm a great asset to the pig farm and she doesn't know what they would do without me." He stopped to consider. "*I* don't know what they would do without me, either."

Christopher Rabbit strolled up. "Hello, Runt. Are you better after your accident?"

"Oh, I'm fine. Not one to let a little thing like a broken leg stop me."

"How are May and Maytwo?" Caravan Bear asked politely.

Runt laughed proudly. "Oh, you know my two girls. Causing trouble as usual. I'd have brought them along but three of us couldn't sit on this bike."

"I don't suppose they could," Christopher Rabbit replied, looking at the ancient motorbike, which seemed about to collapse in a rusty heap under Runt's weight.

Runt climbed down. "It's so good to see you all," he said. "One of Nathan's pigeons told me where you were."

"I thought Nathan didn't like pigeons," said Whitby. ****

"Oh, he doesn't. But they like roosting in the garden centre," Runt replied. He looked around at them. "I've come for a story and a bite to eat. Riding that old thing is hungry work."

He aimed a kick at the motorbike and a piece of metal fell off with a clang.

Caravan Bear and Christopher Rabbit exchanged glances. They had just eaten.

"I'll get Runt something to eat and fetch my Bible," Christopher Rabbit suggested.

"That's a splendid idea," said Runt.

Once Runt had eaten, they all settled down on the grass beside the caravan.

"You said that Jesus walked to a boat across the sea," Whitby reminded Christopher Rabbit. "Why did he do that?"

"Did he really?" asked Runt.

"It wasn't the sea, it was a great lake," Christopher Rabbit told them. "Jesus' friends, the disciples, were in a boat, rowing to the other side."

"Wasn't Jesus with them?" asked Whitby.

"He couldn't have been – otherwise he wouldn't have walked over the water to join them, would he?" asked Hector.

"I suppose not," said Whitby, trying to work it out.

"Where *was* Jesus, then?" Runt asked.

"He had gone up a hill by himself to pray," Christopher Rabbit explained.

"He seemed to spend a lot of time going up hills to pray," Hector said.

"I think," said Caravan Bear slowly, "that if I were as famous as Jesus, always surrounded by crowds, then I'd need to be by myself at times."

"I think Jesus needed to be alone to talk to God," Whitby said decidedly. "Do you think you need to be on your own to talk to God, Christopher Rabbit?"

"I think you can talk to God anywhere and at any time," Christopher Rabbit replied.

"I talk to God all the time," Runt boasted. "Around the farm, in the pigsties, surrounded by other pigs – I'm always talking to God. I don't have to go up hills to do it." He laughed. "I'd be out of breath if I had to go up a hill to talk to him."

"I don't suppose Jesus was," Hector murmured.

Walking on Water

"Well, it might be easier to listen to what God's trying to say if you're on your own, rather than in the middle of a crowd," Christopher Rabbit said mildly.

"I like to be on my own as well," Runt said earnestly. "But it isn't easy when you've got a pig farm to look after for the farmer. Anyway, I'm pretty sure I know what God wants to say to me," he added with confidence.

Christopher Rabbit continued. "Jesus was on the hillside all night, and the boat was a long way from shore. A strong wind had risen and high waves buffeted the little boat this way and that. When Jesus came down to the lakeside, he saw the disciples

rowing as hard as they could, but they weren't getting anywhere."

"Maybe they were worn out," said Whitby.

"I expect they were," Christopher Rabbit agreed. "So Jesus went to help them."

"Did he go in another boat?" asked Runt.

"No, he didn't go in a boat," Christopher Rabbit replied. "Just before dawn, the disciples saw Jesus walk toward them on the lake."

"How do you mean 'walk toward them'?" Runt demanded.

"Didn't he get his feet wet?" Whitby asked.

"Didn't he sink?" Hector chimed in.

"Could he swim?" questioned Caravan Bear.

Christopher Rabbit shook his head. "It just says in the Bible that Jesus walked on the water."

"Wow!" said Whitby.

"I wonder if I could walk on the water," Runt considered thoughtfully.

"I wouldn't think so," Hector replied. "You're not Jesus."

"Jesus must have got his feet wet," Whitby said. "I wonder if he was wearing waterproof boots."

"Didn't they wear sandals in those days?" Hector asked.

"What did Jesus' disciples think when they saw him?" Caravan Bear asked.

"I expect they were terrified," said Hector placidly. "I would have been."

Whitby looked at him. "Nothing frightens you. You're the calmest horse I know."

"How many horses do you know?" Hector replied.

"Well, none really," Whitby admitted. "But nothing seems to scare you. Those boars didn't."

Hector shrugged. "Everyone has things they're scared of," he replied. "You don't like snakes, do you? Or boars."

"I'm not too keen on spiders either," Whitby confessed.

"I'm not scared of anything," Runt boasted.

"Jesus' disciples were terrified," Christopher Rabbit said firmly.

"Told you so," Hector smiled smugly.

"What does scare you, Hector?" Whitby asked curiously.

"Seeing Jesus walk toward me across a lake," Hector replied instantly.

"No, really – what does scare you?" Whitby repeated.

Hector looked away and frowned. "My old master," he said shortly. "He terrified me."

Caravan Bear went up and stroked him. "It's all right," he said gently. "He can't do anything to you now. You're safe with us."

There was a moment's silence.

"So what did the disciples do when they saw Jesus walking on the water?" Caravan Bear asked patiently.

Christopher Rabbit continued. "His disciples thought they were seeing a ghost and cried out in terror. Jesus called to them. 'Don't be afraid! It really is me!' Peter shouted back to him, 'Lord, if it is you, then tell me to come to you on the water!'"

"Why did he do that?" asked Runt.

"Perhaps he wanted to try it," suggested Hector.

Runt wrinkled up his nose as he thought. "If he only wanted to try it for himself, he wouldn't have asked Jesus, would he? He'd just have got out of the boat."

"Would it be because Peter was the sort of person who felt he had to keep proving himself to Jesus?" Caravan Bear wondered.

Christopher Rabbit nodded. "That's right. You remember when Jesus washed his friends' feet at the last supper and Peter was horrified? He asked Jesus to wash all of him, not just his feet. I think he was trying to prove himself then." ****

"But Peter let him down, didn't he? He said he'd never, ever betray Jesus, but he did, three times," Hector added. ****

"There's a word for someone who acts before they think, isn't there?" Runt said. "Imp... something or other. Give me a moment and I'll think of it."

"Do you mean 'impetuous'?" asked Christopher Rabbit.

"That's it! I knew I'd think of it if I tried!"

Christopher Rabbit smiled. "Perhaps Peter loved Jesus and wanted to follow him so much that he

What Jesus Did

sometimes tried a bit too hard," he said thoughtfully. "Anyway, Jesus told Peter to come to him across the lake. Peter stepped carefully out of the boat and began walking on the water. But when a strong gust of wind caught him, he was frightened and began to sink. 'Lord, save me!' he cried."

"And did Jesus?" asked Whitby.

"Of course he did," Hector said scornfully. "Haven't you been listening to *any* of the stories Christopher Rabbit has told us about Jesus?"

"Jesus immediately reached out his hand and caught Peter," Christopher Rabbit said. "'Don't you have enough faith in me, Peter?' he asked. 'Why did

you doubt me?' They climbed into the boat and, at that moment, the wind died down."

"Hooray!" Whitby exclaimed.

"I bet the other disciples in the boat were pretty amazed," Caravan Bear said thoughtfully.

"They were," Christopher Rabbit replied. "One of them said, 'You really are God's Son.'"

"So," Hector argued, "if Peter had had enough faith in Jesus, who is God's Son, he would have been able to walk across the water to Jesus. But because he didn't have enough faith, he could only take a few steps before he began to sink."

Runt jumped up. "I bet I could walk on the water," he said confidently, walking toward the jetty. "I've got loads of faith."

"I don't think..." Caravan Bear began, but it was too late. Runt had gone to the end of the jetty, jumped off, and promptly disappeared!

The friends rushed down the beach.

"He'll drown!" Whitby exclaimed.

But a moment later they saw him swimming toward them.

Runt reached the shore and rejoined them, shaking himself vigorously. Drops of water flew everywhere.

"I can't walk on water," he admitted.

He sat down and beamed at them.

"I didn't know you could swim," Whitby said.

"I didn't know I could either," Runt agreed. He shrugged. "But then I didn't know I could ride a motorbike until I tried."

"I don't think the story is just about walking on water," Caravan Bear said thoughtfully. "Isn't it about putting our trust in Jesus to save us when things go wrong?"

"I think so," Christopher Rabbit agreed, "and not just when things go wrong but all the time." He closed his Bible. "Thank you, God, for the story. And thank you for Peter, who you loved despite his faults. It shows us that you love us with all our faults."

Runt smiled. "I don't think I've got any faults," he said simply.

None of the others could think of an answer to this.

"Sorry I was nasty to you, Whitby," Hector said uncomfortably. "I just like teasing you."

"That's all right," Whitby replied. "I like teasing you back."

They smiled at each other.

"Well," said Runt, getting to his feet. "It's been wonderful meeting you, and I thought the story was great, but I'd better get going."

He put on his goggles and helmet and climbed onto the bike. After a couple of attempts, the bike stuttered to life. With a wave of his trotter Runt roared off up the road, leaving everyone covered in a cloud of dust.

"I think we could all do with a dip in the sea to wash off the dust," said Hector.

And that is what they did.

6

Healing the Sick

It was getting dark when the caravan pulled up onto a small patch of wasteland beside a busy main road. Hector parked it by a redbrick wall covered with graffiti.

"It's not very holiday-like, is it?" Whitby sniffed, looking at the empty plastic bottles and litter strewn around.

"It's only for one night," Caravan Bear said apologetically.

"It was my fault for turning the wrong way," Hector admitted.

Caravan Bear sighed. "I should have given you better directions."

Their surroundings depressed them, and the friends were silent as they set up the caravan.

Christopher Rabbit made a meal and they had just started eating it when they heard loud screeches and howls from the other side of the wall.

"Whatever's that?" asked Whitby, peering out of the window.

Hector put his head in through the door. "Sounds like a fight," he said.

A dark shape illuminated by a streetlamp jumped down from the wall and moved toward them. Whitby gasped and shrank back. As the shape approached, they could see that it was a cat. A very large, ginger cat, limping slowly, dragging one of his back legs behind him. As it came closer, the light streaming out from the caravan showed that the cat's face was covered in scratches, as if it had been attacked by an animal with sharp claws. One of its eyes was almost closed.

"Can we help you?" Caravan Bear asked, climbing down the caravan steps. Christopher Rabbit followed.

The cat looked at them suspiciously but didn't speak.

"Come into the caravan," Christopher Rabbit suggested. "We can give you something to eat and drink."

The cat still said nothing but struggled up the steps and collapsed on a rug.

Caravan Bear fetched a saucer of milk while Christopher Rabbit began cleaning the cat's face.

"Can we do anything about your leg?" Christopher Rabbit asked.

The cat shook his head wearily. "No," he said, speaking in a hoarse whisper. "Did it a week ago. My own fault. Didn't get out of the way in time and a car ran me over." He began lapping the milk thirstily. When the bowl was empty, Caravan Bear filled it up again.

"What about your eye and all those scratches?" Whitby asked. "Did that happen at the same time?"

The cat shook his head again. "Happened just now. Didn't you hear the fight?" He pushed the empty bowl away and sighed. "Great. I needed that."

He looked around at them and his good eye narrowed. "What are you doing here, then?" he asked warily. "Not part of another gang, are you?"

"We're not part of any gang," Caravan Bear assured him. "We're here on holiday."

"Funny place for a holiday," said the cat, unconvinced.

"It's true," Caravan Bear insisted. "We took a wrong turning. Look, we've just started eating and there's plenty if you'd like to share it. And you're welcome to stay the night, if you want."

The cat looked from one to the other, then made up his mind. "OK. Thanks for the offer. My name's Vince."

They all settled down to eat.

"What happened to you?" Whitby asked curiously.

"It was a fight over who's leader of the gang," Vince explained. "I was top cat until I got run over. Now they all want to be boss and push me out." He sighed. "Bad enough trying to keep the other gangs from coming onto our patch without fighting among ourselves."

"Do you have to fight?" asked Whitby. "Can't you just walk away?"

Healing the Sick

Vince shrugged. "Nowhere to go."

"Don't you belong to anyone?" Whitby persisted.

"Used to. Nice lady on the other side of town. But you know how it is – I got fed up with an easy life. Wanted to see places and have adventures." He laughed bitterly. "One night I walked out through the cat flap, got in with a gang, and never went back." He looked around. "Nice little set-up you've got here. Where d'you come from?"

The friends told Vince their names and where they'd been.

After they'd all eaten (and Vince ate a lot as he was very hungry) Caravan Bear and Christopher Rabbit quietly cleared away.

"Christopher Rabbit often reads us a story from the Bible," said Whitby, lying beside Vince on the rug. She felt very sorry for him. "Would you like that?"

Vince shrugged. "Fine by me."

"Tell us about Jesus healing people," Whitby asked Christopher Rabbit.

"All right." Christopher Rabbit fetched his Bible. He turned the pages. "Here's one about a man who couldn't walk."

What Jesus Did

"Bad enough with one dodgy leg out of four," Vince remarked. "Must be worse for humans, who've only got two legs."

"Jesus had come back to Jerusalem for one of the Jewish holy days," Christopher Rabbit began. "Just outside the city was a pool, called the pool of Bethesda. Crowds of sick people lay around it, shaded from the hot sun by some porches. Among them was a man who had not been able to walk for thirty-eight years. Jesus stopped beside him and asked if he'd like to get well."

Healing the Sick

"That's a silly question," Vince broke in. "Of course he'd have liked to get well. I'd like to get well too."

"Not necessarily," said Hector thoughtfully. "The man might have been making a good living from begging."

"I've begged on the streets and it's no joke sleeping rough," Vince replied. "That's how I got in with the gang. I was only little and they said they'd take care of me." He thought for a moment. "Fine care it's proved to be!" he added bitterly.

"But I thought you were the leader?" said Caravan Bear.

"I was. Fought my way to the top. Only way to survive in a gang," Vince answered shortly.

Christopher Rabbit went on with the story. "The sick man told Jesus that he couldn't get well because he didn't have anyone who would put him in the pool when the water bubbled up. He said that someone always got there in front of him."

"What did he mean?" asked Hector.

"I'm not sure," admitted Christopher Rabbit, "but I think it might have meant that people thought that the pool had healing powers and the first person in it when the water began bubbling would be cured of whatever was wrong with them."

Whitby listened to this, wide-eyed.

"Was it true?" she asked.

"I've no idea," said Christopher Rabbit honestly.

Vince laughed. "I can just picture all those sick people fighting each other to be first in the pool!"

"So did Jesus put the lame man into the pool when it began to bubble?" asked Whitby.

"No," Christopher Rabbit replied. "He just said, 'Stand up, pick up your mat, and walk!'"

"Perhaps he thought the man wasn't really lame at all," Vince said, cynically. "Perhaps the man was just trying to deceive people into giving him food."

"I don't think the man would have pretended to be lame for thirty-eight years," Hector said. "Wouldn't have been much of a life, would it?"

"And he couldn't have pretended to his family and friends for all those years," Caravan Bear added.

Vince shrugged. "Perhaps he didn't have any family or friends."

"So what happened?" Whitby asked. "Was it a miracle?"

"The man did as Jesus said. He got up, rolled up his sleeping mat, and began to walk," said Christopher Rabbit.

Everyone was silent while they thought about it.

"Jesus healed other people too, didn't he?" Caravan Bear asked eventually.

"He healed lots of people who had all kinds of sicknesses," Christopher Rabbit replied.

"Tell us another story," Whitby begged.

Christopher Rabbit smiled at him. "All right. One day some people brought a blind man and asked Jesus to touch him."

"Why touch him?" Vince asked.

"Because they had faith that Jesus could help him," Christopher Rabbit said. "And they thought that just his touch would heal the man. Jesus led him away from the crowds to a quiet place outside the village. He gently touched the man's eyes and put his hands on the man's shoulders.

"'Do you see anything?' he asked.

"The man looked around nervously. 'I see people, but everything's misty. They look like big, moving shapes,' he said. 'Like trees walking.'"

"I wonder what it's like to be blind?" Whitby asked. She closed her eyes, got up from the rug, began to walk, and fell over Vince's bad leg. He let out a howl of pain.

"Oh, I'm so sorry, Vince!" she cried, apologetically. "Did I hurt you?"

Healing the Sick

"What do you think?" Vince replied, shifting his position slightly.

"Perhaps the people he could see were his friends, the ones who'd taken the man to Jesus," suggested Hector.

"Could the man see when he was younger?" asked Caravan Bear.

"I've no idea," Christopher Rabbit admitted. "But I expect he could, as otherwise he wouldn't have known what trees looked like, let alone people."

"So what did Jesus do?" asked Hector.

"He touched the man's eyes once more. When he took them away the mist had cleared, and the man could see everything clearly."

"I like hearing about how Jesus healed people," said Whitby happily. "Tell us another one."

"It's getting a bit late," Christopher Rabbit said. "What does everyone else think?"

"I'd like to hear another story," said Vince. "Makes me

think about when I was a kitten and my mother told me stories." A sad look passed across his face. "Don't know what she'd think of me now. I've done some bad things since then."

There was a moment's silence.

"All right," said Christopher Rabbit. "One day a group of people brought their friend to see Jesus. The man was deaf. He couldn't hear and he could barely speak. His friends asked Jesus to cure him.

"Jesus took the man away from the crowd," Christopher Rabbit continued. "He gently touched the man's ears and his tongue. Then he looked up to heaven and said, 'Ephphatha.'"

"What does that mean?" asked Hector.

"It means 'be opened'," Christopher Rabbit replied.

"Why did he look up to heaven?" asked Vince.

"Was he asking God to heal the man?" Caravan Bear asked.

"I think so," Christopher Rabbit said. "All healing comes from God."

"And could the man hear and speak?" asked Vince.

Christopher Rabbit nodded. "Yes.

He could hear and he could speak. Jesus told the man and his friends not to tell anyone what had happened."

"Why didn't he want other people to know?" asked Hector.

"Do you think it could be because he would then have even more people coming to see him?" asked Caravan Bear.

"Perhaps," Christopher Rabbit agreed. "But the man and his friends did talk about it, of course, and everyone they spoke to was amazed."

"I'm not surprised," said Vince. "I'd be amazed if Jesus knocked on the door of this caravan and healed my leg." He shifted uncomfortably.

"Is it hurting you?" asked Whitby.

"Nothing I can't cope with," said Vince, but he was obviously in pain.

"What will you do?" asked Christopher Rabbit gently. "Go back to the gang?"

"What else can I do?" Vince replied.

"What about the lady you lived with?"

Vince thought about it, then shrugged. "She won't want me now. She's probably nailed up the cat flap."

He looked at them. "Don't worry about me. I'm tough. I'll survive."

"Does she live far away?" asked Caravan Bear suddenly.

"Other side of town," Vince said quickly.

"We could always go that way tomorrow if you like. It's worth a try."

There was silence.

"Why would you want to bother with me?" Vince asked at last.

No one spoke and they went to bed soon after. Before Christopher Rabbit went to sleep, he looked out of the window at the streetlamp shining in on him.

"Please, God, help Vince," he thought. "You don't just heal people's bodies, you heal every part of them, inside and out. Thank you for the stories about how Jesus made sick people well again and gave them a new start with new hope."

The following morning, Hector towed the caravan

across town. As they approached the street, Vince became increasingly nervous.

"This is the place," he told Hector, who stopped in front of a house with a bright blue door.

"Won't be any good," Vince muttered. "She'll probably throw me out when she sees my ugly face."

"We'll wait," Caravan Bear promised.

They watched as Vince took a deep breath before slowly climbing down the steps, crossing the pavement, and pushing at the cat flap. It opened and Vince stepped inside and disappeared.

It was a long wait.

"Do you think we ought to move on?" Hector asked. "There's a sign saying we shouldn't park here and the road's very narrow."

"Just a minute longer," said Caravan Bear, watching the cat flap.

It had been more than a minute and cars, trying to pass, were hooting angrily when the cat flap moved slightly, opened wide, and first a paw, then Vince's head emerged. He waved his paw, a beaming smile on his face, called out "Thank you!" and disappeared back into the house.

What Jesus Did

"Thank *you*, God," said Christopher Rabbit.

"We'd better disappear too before we get arrested," Hector said, as he moved out into the traffic.

Christopher Rabbit sat with Caravan Bear and Whitby on the front step of the caravan as they made their way down the street.

"Do you know where we're going?" Hector called back.

"No, but it doesn't matter," Caravan Bear replied, a beaming smile on his face.

They were all smiling as they rode out of town.

7

Raising the Dead

"Raining again!" said Whitby in disgust as she sat huddled close to Caravan Bear on the front step of the caravan.

"Nothing wrong with a bit of rain," Hector shouted, water dripping off his nose. He began to go faster and the caravan bounced along behind him, splashing through puddles on the road.

"Not so fast!" yelled Whitby. "We're getting soaked!"

"I'm only trying to get to that patch of blue sky just ahead," Hector called, not slowing down.

Christopher Rabbit watched the scenery flash past. The leaves were starting to turn brown and fall from the trees. Autumn, he thought, catching a leaf as it was blown past him. It would soon be time to go home.

He sighed. Although he loved his home, he did enjoy being away in the caravan, having adventures with his friends. He wiped a raindrop from his head and looked around.

"Aren't we somewhere near the garden centre?" he asked.

"Yes," Caravan Bear replied. "I thought it would be nice to call in and see Nathan." ****

"And the gnomes," Whitby added.

When they reached the garden centre, Hector stopped in surprise. Under the sign "Jubbly's Farm and Garden Centre" was a notice that said "For Sale".

Hector turned in through the open gates. "Hello!" he called. "Is anyone there?"

After a moment or two, a black cockerel emerged. It was Nathan. His brilliant red-brown neck feathers and bright red crest had been flattened by the rain. But it wasn't just that, Christopher Rabbit thought as he watched him. He looked sad and miserable, very different from the proud bird they had last met.

"Oh," Nathan said, "it's you. I suppose you want to stay for the night."

"Not if it's any trouble," Caravan Bear replied.

Nathan didn't respond. He stalked off and Hector followed, pulling the caravan into the walled garden. The last time they had come, it had been full of plants for sale. Now there were just a few tired-looking potted trees huddled in one corner. In another corner stood the gnomes. Rows and rows of them had been for sale, looking bright and shining with fresh paint. Now they looked dull and chipped and a few had fallen over.

"Park where you like," Nathan said in a dispirited voice and began to walk away.

"What's happened?" Caravan Bear called after him.

Nathan stopped. "Mr Jubbly's not been well and Mrs Jubbly can't cope on her own. That's why it's up for sale."

"I'm so sorry," said Caravan Bear.

Nathan shrugged. "Well, that's life, but it's not easy to see this place dying."

"Perhaps a new buyer will want to keep you," Hector said encouragingly.

"Perhaps," Nathan replied, unconvinced. "Anyway, you get set up and I'll come and see you later." His voice changed as he spotted two pigeons flying down to perch on the heads of a couple of gnomes. "And if I have to tell you pigeons one more time…!" he shouted in much his old manner.

"Yah, can't catch us!" the pigeons retorted, flying around the gnomes.

Nathan shrugged. "See what it's like here? Everything's gone to rack and ruin."

Once he had gone, the friends set up the caravan in silence, shaken by the change in Nathan. They had supper and settled down.

"At least the rain's stopped," Whitby remarked.

It was still light when Nathan returned.

"Are you going to read a story from the Bible?" he asked Christopher Rabbit. "I'd like to hear one. Take my mind off things."

Christopher Rabbit picked up the Bible from the shelf where it lived. He opened the book and began to read. "Apart from his disciples, Jesus had three close friends, who lived in a village called Bethany, which was a few miles from Jerusalem in a country called Judea," he began. "There were two sisters, Mary and Martha, and a brother called Lazarus. Lazarus became ill and his sisters sent a message to Jesus, telling him that their brother was very unwell."

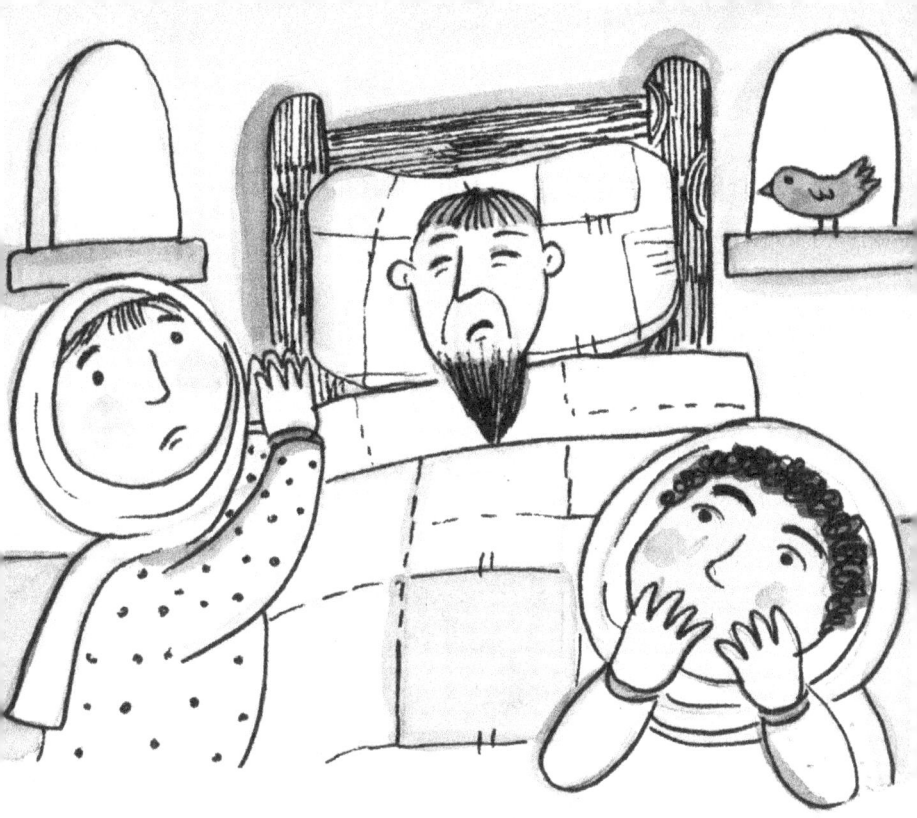

"Mrs Jubbly telephoned their son," Nathan interrupted. "But he lives a long way away and hasn't come to visit."

"Was Jesus a long way away from his friends in Bethany?" asked Whitby.

"I think so," Christopher Rabbit replied. "He was travelling around with his disciples, teaching people about God and healing the sick."

"I suppose they didn't have telephones in those days," Whitby murmured.

"Or emails or cars or planes or anything like that," Hector added.

"So how did they send a message?" Whitby demanded.

"Perhaps by pigeon post," said Nathan angrily, looking over to the pigeons who were darting in between the gnomes. "I told you to clear off!" he roared. The pigeons just laughed and flapped their wings.

"Perhaps they sent one of their neighbours to find Jesus. However it reached him, when Jesus got the message, he said that Lazarus' sickness wouldn't end in his death," Christopher Rabbit continued. "He said it would bring glory to God and his Son. He didn't go back to Bethany to see Lazarus but stayed where he was."

"Why?" asked Nathan. "I'd have thought that Jesus would have rushed to see his friend, especially as he healed sick people. I must admit that I've been very disappointed in Mr and Mrs Jubbly's son. He might live a long way away, but he should have come to see his father."

Christopher Rabbit went on. "Jesus stayed where he was for two days before telling his disciples that they would go to Bethany. His friends weren't very happy about this. One of them reminded Jesus that people in Judea had tried to stone him."

"That wouldn't have stopped Jesus, would it?" Caravan Bear asked. "Jesus wasn't afraid of anything."

"I don't know," Christopher Rabbit replied. "I think there were times when Jesus was afraid, but he carried on doing God's work even when he was scared. He knew that God would always be with him. On their way back to Bethany, Jesus told his disciples that Lazarus had fallen asleep but that he would wake him up."

"Mr Jubbly has been sleeping a lot of the time," Nathan said, nodding his head. "The doctor told Mrs Jubbly that it was a good sign."

"That's also what the disciples said to Jesus," Christopher Rabbit agreed. "They told him that it was good that Lazarus was sleeping as it must mean that he would get better. But Jesus didn't mean the sort of sleep we have when we're tired. He meant that Lazarus had died."

"How did he know?" Whitby demanded.

Christopher Rabbit shrugged. "I don't know."

"I expect God told him," Hector said.

"So Jesus made it clear that Lazarus wasn't asleep but dead," Christopher Rabbit continued. "He said that he was glad they had delayed for two days as what he was going to do would help them to believe in him."

Hector shook his head. "I don't understand."

"Neither did his disciples," Christopher Rabbit replied.

A loud *toot-toot* of a horn interrupted them. It was followed by a scream of tyres as Runt drove in on his motorbike. He narrowly missed the wall, but ended up skidding into the garden gnomes, knocking them over as he screeched to a stop. Nathan rushed over and began picking the gnomes up.

"Hello, hello," Runt shouted, taking off his crash helmet. "Shouldn't leave those gnomes lying around, Nathan. Bit of a hazard." He turned to Christopher Rabbit. "Not too late for the story, am I?"

"I've already started telling it…" Christopher Rabbit began.

"That's all right. I'll soon pick it up," Runt said happily. "I pick things up very quickly. But before you start, do you have anything to eat? Riding this heap of rust makes me very hungry."

Caravan Bear sighed and went into the caravan, returning with a large slice of cake. Runt's eyes gleamed.

"My favourite!" He took a big bite and turned to Christopher Rabbit. "What have I missed?"

"I was telling the story of Lazarus."

"Who's he?" Runt asked, his mouth full.

"A friend of Jesus who was dying," Hector explained.

"A friend of Jesus who had just died," Whitby corrected. "Jesus wasn't there even though his sisters had sent him a message, asking him to come."

"Just like Mr and Mrs Jubbly's son, who hasn't come to see Mr Jubbly even though Mrs Jubbly phoned him," said Nathan.

"How is Mr Jubbly?" Runt asked, eating the last bit of cake.

Nathan shook his head. "Not good."

"To tell you the story so far," Hector said firmly. "It seemed that Jesus was glad he had delayed going until Lazarus had died. He told his friends that then they would have to believe in him."

Runt looked at Christopher Rabbit. "What did he mean by that?"

"You'll see in a minute," said Christopher Rabbit. "When Jesus and his disciples arrived in Bethany, they found that Lazarus had been buried for four days. The house was crowded with friends and neighbours who had come to say how sorry they were. When Martha heard that Jesus had come, she went out to meet him. 'Lord,' she said, 'if you'd been here, my brother wouldn't have died.'"

"Why not?" Runt asked.

"Because Jesus would have saved him," Whitby said.

"Jesus said to her that Lazarus would rise again," Christopher Rabbit continued. "He told her, 'Those who believe in me will live, even though they die, and whoever lives by believing in me will never die.'

He asked Martha if she believed what he'd just said."

"I'm not sure I quite follow that," Nathan said cautiously.

"Oh, I think it's quite simple," Runt said confidently. "Surely it means that if you really believe that Jesus is God's Son, then although you won't live forever on earth, you will live forever in heaven with God."

Everyone looked at Runt in amazement.

"That's pretty neat," said Whitby, impressed.

Christopher Rabbit smiled. "Martha said that she did believe that Jesus was God's Son, the promised saviour. She ran to tell her sister that Jesus had arrived. Mary and their friends came out of the house. Mary was crying. When Jesus saw her, he was very sad."

"I can't think why," said Runt, "as he'd deliberately stayed away."

Christopher Rabbit considered this. "I think Jesus was doing what God wanted him to, but it still upset him to see how sad his friends were. Everyone started crying."

"Even Jesus?" asked Whitby.

"Even Jesus," Christopher Rabbit replied.

"Don't hold with it myself," Nathan said firmly. "Look at me – the garden centre is going to be sold, the pigeons are taking more and more liberties, and I'm likely to be out of a job very soon, but you don't catch me crying." He sniffed.

There was an uncomfortable silence.

After a while, Christopher Rabbit went on. "Jesus asked Mary where they had put Lazarus and she led him to the cave where they had put his body. A large stone had been rolled across the entrance. When he saw it, Jesus said, 'Take away the stone.'"

Nathan pulled a face. "If he's been dead for four days, he'd have begun to rot."

"That's what Martha said," Christopher Rabbit agreed. "Jesus replied, 'Didn't I tell you that if you believe, you will see the wonderful power of God's love?'

"So they did what Jesus asked and took away the stone. Jesus looked up at the sky. 'Father God, thank you for having heard me. I know that you always hear me, but I am asking you now, so that everyone here may believe that you sent me.' Then he called out in a loud voice, 'Come out, Lazarus!'"

"And did he?" Whitby asked.

"Yes. Lazarus came out, still dressed in the grave clothes he'd been buried in."

"That sends shivers down my back," Whitby whispered. "It was a big miracle, wasn't it?"

"Did Jesus turn up late deliberately so that when he raised Lazarus from the dead, everyone watching would believe that he really was God's Son?" asked Runt.

Christopher Rabbit nodded. "That's how it seemed to his friends. Now that Lazarus was alive again, they could understand why Jesus decided not to come to Bethany as soon as he got the message."

"What happened next?" asked Whitby.

"He told Martha and Mary to take off the grave clothes and take Lazarus home," Christopher Rabbit replied.

No one spoke for a while. Then Runt stood up and stretched himself.

"That was a good story and now *I* must be off home – if the motorbike doesn't fall to bits on the way." He turned to Nathan.

"Perhaps Mr Jubbly will get better, but if not, I'm sure there'll be a job for you at the pig farm."

Nathan didn't look as if he liked the idea very much, but he went off looking a bit happier.

Runt put on his crash helmet and rode off with a splutter and a roar of the engine, knocking over another couple of gnomes which stood in his way – much to the delight of the pigeons perched on the wall.

"That's a funny thing," said Whitby watching him go. "I wouldn't have thought Runt would have been bothered about Nathan. I thought he only cared about himself."

"I don't know," Christopher Rabbit said thoughtfully.

"Perhaps he's learned something from the Bible stories," said Caravan Bear.

"Perhaps," Christopher Rabbit agreed. As he put the Bible back on the shelf, he said, "Thank you, God, for the story of how Jesus raised Lazarus from the dead. Please help Mr and Mrs Jubbly and Nathan know that you care for them and give them hope for the future."

"And that you care for Runt," Whitby added, surprisingly.

Christopher Rabbit smiled at him. "And that you care for Runt and for all of us."

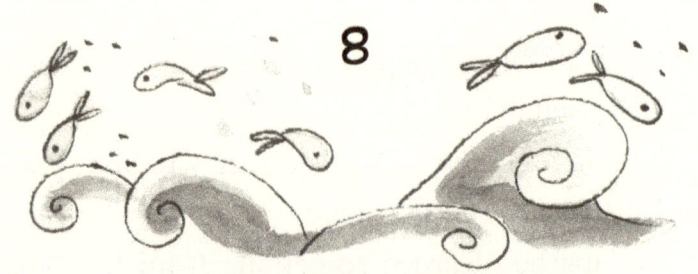

A Meal with Friends

"You said ages ago that we could go fishing – and now it's the end of our holiday and we haven't been," Whitby said sadly.

Caravan Bear clapped his paw to his forehead. "I'm so sorry, Whitby – I clean forgot." He leaned forward and called out. "Hector, could you pull off here by the river?"

"Why? We're not far from Christopher Rabbit's burrow."

"I haven't taken Whitby fishing and I promised."

Caravan Bear turned to Christopher Rabbit. "Do you mind if we stay here tonight?"

"I'd love it," Christopher Rabbit replied.

So Hector turned off the road and parked the caravan on a bank beside the river. It was a bright, sunny day and Caravan Bear, Whitby, and Christopher Rabbit were soon happily fishing.

Suddenly they were drenched by a large wave!

"Hello! Oh, sorry about that! I didn't mean to splash you, but I've caught a crab!"

The voice came from a brown water rat, who was standing in a brightly painted green and blue boat, looking at them worriedly while he tried to drag one of his oars out of some mud.

Whitby jumped up and shook herself. Drops of water flew everywhere.

The water rat gave one great heave of his oar, which flew out of the mud and toppled him over backward.

"Oh dear," he said, getting up, "I always forget about mud at this spot."

"What does 'catching a crab' mean?" Whitby asked.

"It means putting your oar in the water at the wrong time or at the wrong angle, or digging it in too deeply – which is what I've just done. My mind was on other things."

The water rat rowed to the shore and stepped out.

"So sorry about splashing you. I do apologize. You're not too wet, are you?"

"Oh no," Caravan Bear said, wiping his paw across his damp head. "It's a fine day and we'll soon dry off."

A Meal with Friends

"Then may I introduce myself?" asked the water rat. "I'm Walter, and very pleased to meet you. It's not often one comes across a bear, a rabbit, and a dog fishing in the river. In fact," he added wrinkling up his face, "it's not often one sees a bear, a rabbit, and a dog all at the same time." He looked past them, squinting in the sun. "And is that a horse?"

"That's Hector," Caravan Bear replied. "He doesn't fish."

"He just eats," Whitby interrupted.

Caravan Bear frowned at her. "I'm Caravan Bear, this is Christopher Rabbit, and this is Whitby."

"How splendid," Walter replied. "I feel I know you already. This is going to be a good day." He beamed at them. "Are you on holiday?"

"Yes. It's our last day and I've caught three fish," Whitby told him proudly.

Walter blinked. "How splendid."

"We're in our caravan," Whitby confided.

"A caravan! How wonderful! I'm sorry to be ignorant – but what is a caravan?"

"Come and see," Caravan Bear invited. "It's just along the bank."

When Walter reached the caravan, he clapped his paws together. "Oh my! Gosh! How absolutely fantastic!"

Caravan Bear swelled with pride. "Won't you stay and have some lunch?" he asked.

"Oh really? Thank you. I'd love to," Walter said happily.

"And you tow this caravan, do you?" he asked Hector.

Hector nodded.

"You must be very strong."

It was Hector's turn to swell with pride. "I do my best," he said with unusual modesty.

Walter looked from one to the other. "You're all amazing," he said.

"Christopher Rabbit tells us stories from the Bible," Whitby told him. "He really makes them come alive."

"Does he really?" Walter beamed. "I'd love to hear one."

"And I don't do anything at all," Whitby said hurriedly.

"You seem to be quite good at catching fish," Walter told her.

The friends all warmed to the small brown water rat.

"Do you live on the river?" Christopher Rabbit asked as they sat down to eat.

"On it, beside it, and in it," Walter replied.

"And that's your boat?" Caravan Bear asked.

"It is indeed. I built her myself and today is my very first trip out. She's my pride and joy," Walter replied.

"That's how I feel about the caravan," Caravan Bear agreed.

Lunch was a happy affair and afterward Walter took Caravan Bear, Christopher Rabbit, and Whitby out on the water.

Hector wandered along the bank, keeping pace with the small boat as Walter rowed slowly along the shoreline, past thick banks of reeds, past trailing branches of willow trees, past ducks and swans busy about their business.

"There's nothing in life as good as messing about in boats," Walter said dreamily, gently dipping the oars in and out of the water. "Just messing about…"

It was a lovely afternoon and they thanked Walter profusely when he pulled in to the shore.

"Do you have to go straight away?" asked Christopher Rabbit hesitantly. "Only if you don't, perhaps you'd like me to read a story from the Bible."

"Yes please," Walter said enthusiastically.

"It's about fishing, actually," Christopher Rabbit explained. "And friendship."

"Really? How amazing!" Walter exclaimed.

A Meal with Friends

Everyone settled down. Before he began to read, Christopher Rabbit looked around his friends and sighed. Soon he'd be home and although he'd be glad to see Min and Henry and all his friends, he'd miss Caravan Bear, Whitby, and Hector.

He looked at Walter, who was gazing at him expectantly. Christopher Rabbit's whiskers twitched and he began to read. "This story takes place after Jesus had been killed, but had risen from the dead," he explained.

"Was he a ghost, then?" asked Walter. "My grandmother believes in ghosts. I don't. At least, I might if I saw one, but I never have."

"I wouldn't like to see a ghost," said Whitby, shivering.

"No, Jesus wasn't a ghost," Christopher Rabbit explained. "When he appeared to his disciples, he was real."

"Oh good," said Walter. "I don't like ghost stories."

Christopher Rabbit went on. "Jesus had told his disciples to go back to Galilee, and he would meet them there. So that's what they did."

"What were they going to do?" asked Caravan Bear. "They'd seen Jesus killed, then seen him alive. They knew he was the Son of God. Had he told them what he wanted them to do next?"

"I don't think so," Christopher Rabbit said, "because when they met beside the great lake, the place where they'd first met Jesus, Peter said he was going fishing."

"Perhaps he was hungry," said Whitby.

Christopher Rabbit went on. "The others decided to join him, so they got into their boat and rowed far out."

"Because Jesus hadn't told them what he wanted them to do, perhaps they just thought they'd go back to being fishermen," Caravan Bear wondered.

A Meal with Friends

"Must have been a bit of a let-down after all that had happened to them," Hector remarked.

"They fished all night but didn't catch anything," Christopher Rabbit went on.

"We fished all morning, and I caught three and Christopher Rabbit caught one," Whitby said proudly.

"And I didn't catch anything," Caravan Bear sighed.

"Sometimes the fish just won't bite," Walter replied sympathetically.

"When it began to get light, they started rowing back to shore," Christopher Rabbit continued. "They saw a man standing at the water's edge. He shouted to them, 'Have you caught anything?'

"'No,' they shouted back. 'Throw your net over the right-hand side of the boat and you will!' the man called."

"It was Jesus, wasn't it?" Whitby said, wriggling happily.

Christopher Rabbit smiled at her. "Yes, it was Jesus, but the disciples didn't recognize him."

"Why not?" asked Caravan Bear.

Christopher Rabbit shrugged. "I don't know. Perhaps it was a misty morning and they couldn't see him clearly.

"They did what Jesus suggested and they caught so many fish that they had trouble hauling the net into the boat. Then Peter suddenly realized who it was. 'It's the Lord!' he shouted, and jumped over the side."

"He didn't try walking on the water, did he?" asked Whitby.

"No. He just swam for the shore. The disciples rowed the boat back to land. When they got there, they found that Jesus had made a fire and was cooking breakfast. There was fresh bread and the smell of grilled fish."

Hector wrinkled his nose. "It's funny, but somehow I can't imagine Jesus doing something as ordinary as cooking a meal."

"Why not?" asked Caravan Bear.

"Well, he's too important. You don't expect the Son of God to cook breakfast – I don't, anyway."

"There's nothing as good as eating breakfast early in the morning after a spell of fishing," Walter

A Meal with Friends

remarked. "They all must have been hungry."

"I expect they were," Christopher Rabbit agreed.

"And happy," Whitby said. "I bet they were happy. You said that perhaps they didn't know what to do after Jesus had told them to go to Galilee, but now

that Jesus was with them everything would be all right, wouldn't it?"

Christopher Rabbit nodded. "Jesus told them to come and eat breakfast and bring some of the fish they'd just caught. They dragged the full net of fish up on to the shore."

"Did they count the fish?" asked Walter.

"They'd caught a hundred and fifty-three."

Whitby blinked. "I've only been able to catch three – apart from the one that got eaten by a duck."

"Didn't the net break under the weight?" Hector asked.

Christopher Rabbit shook his head. "No. They joined Jesus at the fire but none of them asked who he was."

"Of course they didn't," said Hector, impatiently. "They knew it was Jesus. Who else would it have been? The owner of the local fish and chip shop?"

"Jesus took the bread and fish he'd cooked and gave it to them," Christopher Rabbit went on.

"Did he thank God for it first, like he did when he fed five thousand people?" asked Whitby.

"I'm sure he did."

A Meal with Friends

"A better meal than five loaves and two little fish," Hector muttered.

"When they'd all eaten, Jesus took Peter off by himself. 'Peter, do you love me more than these others do?' he asked him. Peter replied, 'Yes, Lord, you know I love you.'"

"Why did he ask Peter that?" asked Caravan Bear. "He knew that Peter loved him."

Christopher Rabbit thought for a moment. "Of course Jesus knew it. But he also knew that Peter had made mistakes and probably felt guilty about them."

"You mean like the time Peter said he didn't know him after Jesus had been arrested?" asked Caravan Bear. ****

Christopher Rabbit nodded.

"Why did Jesus take Peter away from the other disciples?" asked Whitby.

"I think it was a kind thing to do," said Walter. "If you're going to tell someone off, it's nicer not to do it in front of others."

Whitby wrinkled her nose. "But Jesus didn't tell him off, did he? He just asked Peter if he loved him."

What Jesus Did

Christopher Rabbit went on. "Jesus said to him, 'Feed my lambs.'"

"Why did he say that?" asked Walter, confused. "You've not mentioned sheep before."

"Didn't Jesus think of people as being like sheep?" asked Hector. "With him as the good shepherd?"

"Jesus asked Peter a second time whether he loved him. When Peter again said that he did, Jesus said, 'Tend my sheep.'"

"What does that mean?" asked Whitby.

"It means look after them, care for them," Caravan Bear replied.

A Meal with Friends

Christopher Rabbit went on. "Jesus asked Peter the same question a third time and Peter replied. 'You know everything. You know, Lord, that I love you.' And Jesus told him to feed his sheep."

Walter looked puzzled. "Why ask the same question three times?"

"Could it be because Peter had said three times that he didn't know Jesus?" asked Caravan Bear.

"It might have been," Christopher Rabbit replied. "Perhaps he was giving Peter the chance to make right all the things that he felt guilty about, the things he was ashamed of, the mistakes he'd made. Perhaps Jesus was saying that despite everything, he still believed in Peter and trusted him to lead the other disciples in carrying on the work of bringing God's kingdom to everyone." He closed his book.

Everyone was quiet for a moment.

"And isn't that what is important for all of us?" asked Caravan Bear. "That he's kind and loving when we mess things up?"

"And goes on believing in us," Hector added.

"I don't know why God should trust me," said Whitby. "I'm always doing naughty things."

"Well," said Walter, getting to his feet. "It's been wonderful meeting you, and I thought the story was terrific, but I really must be going. Mustn't be late for this evening's performance."

"What performance?" Caravan Bear asked.

"Oh, I thought you must have known. I'm in a small band – we call ourselves *The Water Rats* – and we play up and down the river during the summer. We're playing tonight just along the shore. You must come along."

"We'd love to," said Whitby enthusiastically. "Caravan Bear plays the guitar, you know."

A Meal with Friends

"Not very well," Caravan Bear said hurriedly. "What sort of music do you play?"

"Water music, of course."

With a friendly wave, Walter jumped into his boat and rowed off.

That evening Christopher Rabbit, Caravan Bear, Whitby, and Hector walked along the riverbank. When they reached the spot where the concert would take place, they found it was fast filling up with excited animals and birds. Among them came Christopher Rabbit's friends from home. Min the cat, Susie the squirrel, and Frank the mole arrived first, followed by the beavers Henry and Maisie and their sons, who were staggering under the weight of a large picnic hamper. Slowly following some way behind was Albert the badger.

"How lovely to see you!" Maisie said, giving Christopher Rabbit a hug. "Lantwit told us about this concert and we wondered whether you'd be here. There's plenty of food for all of us."

They settled down to a good meal and a good talk. Then the concert began and the animals listened, spellbound, as *The Water Rats* played to them from a boat moored a little way out.

Christopher Rabbit lay back on the grass beside his friends and watched the moon rise and the stars come out. The sound of the music floated across the water.

"Thank you, God," he thought, "for this wonderful world and this wonderful life. Thank you for all the stories in the Bible, which help us learn a bit more about you. Thank you for Jesus, who came to show us how much you love and care for us and how you go on believing in us even when we mess things up. And thank you, especially, for all the good friends I have. I'm such a lucky rabbit."

* * * * *

The following morning, Caravan Bear harnessed Hector to the caravan and they set off on the road home. Walter and his friends waved them off until the red caravan with yellow wheels had disappeared into the distance. All they could hear was the faint sound of singing:

WHAT JESUS DID

"Clip clop, clip clop,
Travelling fast or travelling slow,
Look very hard and you might see it go:
The bright caravan on the road.
Clip clop, clip clop,
Caravan Bear and all of his friends,
Hector and Whitby, and Rabbit as well,
Off for adventure, off for some fun,
Off for adventure, out in the sun.
Clip clop, clip clop, clip, clip clop."

A Meal with Friends

Other titles by Avril Rowlands

Now available as an audiobook:

More audiobooks from *The Animals' Caravan* series available soon.